The Calamitous Chronicle of
Mr. Livingston
and *Tiger Lily*

poetry by Melissa Booey

Gatekeeper press

The views and opinions expressed in this book are solely those of the author and do not reflect the views or opinions of Gatekeeper Press. Gatekeeper Press is not to be held responsible for and expressly disclaims responsibility for the content herein.

Birdbrain/The Calamitous Chronicle of Mr. Livingston and Tiger Lily

Published by Gatekeeper Press
7853 Gunn Hwy, Suite 209
Tampa, FL 33626
www.GatekeeperPress.com

Copyright © 2023 by Melissa Booey

All rights reserved. Neither this book, nor any parts within it may be sold or reproduced in any form or by any electronic or mechanical means, including information storage and retrieval systems, without permission in writing from the author. The only exception is by a reviewer, who may quote short excerpts in a review.

The cover design, typesetting, and editorial work for this book are entirely the product of the author. Gatekeeper Press did not participate in and is not responsible for any aspect of these elements.

Illustrations by Betsy Wojcinski and Ashley Munson

ISBN (paperback): 9781662929458
eISBN: 9781662929465

When Tiger Lily first ran her ship aground, Mr. Livingston dragged her from the wreckage and brought her back to life. A handsome gentle-wolf and a ruined rapscallion, they traded tales and adventures of the mountains and sea.

He longed to make his way back up the hillside, to take her dancing by the lake. She couldn't bear the thought of sailing on without him.

One of sand, and one of sea,
Mr. Livingston and Tiger Lily: quite calamitous, indeed.

nectar

One day your flowers may die
probably soon
I will be sad

Someone else may bring me flowers
that might be nice
they would be beautiful...

It will mean nothing.

landslide

In that moment
paralleled only by the other
in this vast expanded nowhereland
this prescribed hypnosis
seemingly stranded between dispelled limbos
stretching breathless fingertips across nothing-ed hemispheres
to find that still familiar constant

even you
ever bright shining in politely garnished inner disquiet
saw
dead leaves falling as graceless star-stained moons
and the truly recognizable atmosphere of
utter amnesiacs wandering
wherein you had already begun toward somewhere in the distance
turning round and away from my blistering advancement

in that same place my heart whispered
between beats of ironed out pretend:

"he has already forgotten you!"

rosewater

In a faraway February
you sat with me at the edge of a hotel bed
we dreamt big dreams in downtown la la land
held each other closer than we thought possible
you called me captivating

I sat in a jumbled heap of metal not one week later
you wheeled me around and kept me company
kicking yourself for my carnage

These shipwrecks were only an indication of the
ghost voyage to come

I do hope you made it to the other side

fog

I keep expecting you to call, or write, or show up at
my door like some lost puppy
I'm the one waiting in the rain
left outside, covered in dust as raindrops
try try try to get my number
I stand there clutching golf clubs you've abandoned
        just like me
I remember when you were a giant, larger than the life
I'd meant to lead, that wouldn't couldn't should not
keep me honest

Now I see you are a blip on the radar
        blood-spotted milk and worm-fed apples in my garden
            but not really
                  such things will never be true for us

you and me.

Forever my world that got away
my dislodged subterranean paradise
my ruptured hemisphere
        You are the hole in my head I have to live with
the cranial oozing of matter I'll never repair
the scar I'll have to keep in style
every season, every time they tell that joke
I didn't get the first time, or remind me of that
poorly purchased gold broach I never wear

I never liked you half as much as I loved you.

It had been raining and storming, the sea violent and furious. Tiger Lily had run out into the night, wanting it to devour her. Mr. Livingston had always followed, through the sea and the squalls and the deadliest tides.

But he was finally exhausted.

As she battered away, daring the waves to take her, he fell into a deep sleep. He dreamt of warm summer days chopping wood by the river, and fresh mountain air through the trees. He had grown weary of salty air, of the sun beating down on his face.

He wished for it to be still, and quiet…

bloodstone

You will always win
You will always survive me

You drove me into the desert drinking sand water and
breathing back old sins, I was your shade,
yet you dehydrated my sunshine

You magnified my seas

I couldn't see
that there was land worth making it back to
relying on your mirage
once you saw
I could exist independently
of your unquenchable glory

You were a wasteland for my nerves

I tried to fit the mold
make my seizures more attractive
tried to make post traumatic tremors more capable
of smoking smiles and pretty faces
hosting parties like I meant it
both frauds
I'll admit it

yet you will outlive me.

gasoline

You were the kid that saved snails I was the kid who smashed them I
think it's always meant to be Even if for single breaths of history
there were moments when you looked at me and I briefly believed it
was "forever" maybe just maybe Then there were times I wanted you to
perish in a fire There was a pregnant pause and I could swear you started
the engine-could have sworn you didn't check under the car
for a sleeping kitten just trying to keep warm on another cold winter
morning on the wrong side of town once the metal chokes and
squeals to life that defenseless fur ball is swallowed whole Now that
kitten was my heart and you were the Oldsmobile too tired to check under
your hood for that sleeping danger you just fed yesterday got tired of
cleaning the litter box "accidentally" left the door open-not
such a humanitarian anymore are you It's those little things we can't
hide from those dead ends are so addictive That same atrophy that
familiar back door the alleyway housing grown-up monsters In a way these
things are comforting when you get used to all the darkness

and the darkness is forgiving It's the sunlight that will get you It's the bright spots that consume you It's that sick hope like a needle you inject it like a drug but it gets you back to nowhere back to comfy dead-end city where your dreams remind your nightmares that this is better than nothing right? It's better than those shmucks who got their happy ever after Suckers right Yeah That's it It's always cooler being the kid with the cigarette stuck in their windpipe refusing to learn your lessons is still in style the people want to hear how we have failed it will help to know that some of us never do anything with the mess That we are the mess We are every inch of the disaster the lesson is a brick through the passenger windshield Your hysterics bring nobody back Still the memories remain in my birdbrain and after this much time I can promise everyone involved that the trouble is not worthwhile and the instinctual bloodstain you tried to bleach un-wild never came out anyway just grew into a causeway that escorts us back and forth across the wreckage

quicksand

I hope a wave train
soaks your soul
while you're standing outside of the synagogue

floods your family campfire
ruins that hot date

whiskey tea

I am a lonely shopping cart

It's getting so I can't picture
high tops in my entryway
worn down sneakers on the carpet
did you miss the whole point of taking them off?

I miss the debris
so proud of yourself for making the bed

Here I am picking on you from lightyears away
from a place that no longer exists

Not much has changed on my end
still clutching my bottle bred insomnia and
my once prized smoker's cough.

Tiger Lily had loved hearing about the mountaintop Mr. Livingston held so close to his heart; he said it was the only place he felt at home.

He'd promised to take her there one day.

Alone and reflective, she now looks out at the sea, scribbling away in her journal: "There are days when the rain hits the palms and I pretend that they're pines, and I can smell the Yosemite wilderness on a crisp, spring morning. I can smell freshly cut wood in a roaring fire and Irish whiskey poured ...

.... I can almost smell you."

saltwater

I can't wait to feel nothing for you,
you left me with nothing but this feeling

you should be fading from my aching ever-consciousness
body burnt and head cut off to make certain your corpse
won't come for me years after the massacre

I fear that inevitable day
when I hear your wedding announcement on the lips of someone else
a random run-in to finish shattering my world
leaving me to dance with your phantom and
bribe crypt keepers for hours at your graveside

breathe in those deep gulps of well-deserved freedom
I'm no longer your task

the job we planned on applying for became
the last position we'd ever want to hold together

Time is the narcissist
the evidence is daunting.

moon rocks

You're still my favorite when I'm not sooing clearly

My smitten, cross-eyed epidemic always on the case
        bathing me in gallons of barrel-aged chagrin
        swallowing my tissue to preserve

                                         my blood, my brain, my

bones

I wonder how we remain intrigued by your
impersonations, your bootleg routines,
your 10 out of 10 impressions.
In no particular order, we still marvel at you, we do.

You're so charming and easy to pet like the
        lovable family pup
                living on in legacy
                        buried in the backyard

old chain collar and tags hanging up in dad's office

I felt guilty throwing yours away

bathwater

Didn't you once love these soft, sweet hands-
this pair of feet?
To think they are no longer yours to hold, and kiss, and treat.
Now I keep them numb by daily whiskey-rinse-repeat,
while commissioning the shadows to descend on fresher meat.

kidney stone

Thinking of you now is
         knowing you aren't mine to straddle
making me purr from every pore on my body

those cloudy eyes that hit me like a rogue wave as your
         need pulled me close
naps and blanket forts for afternoon delights

      too much hung in the balance

the empty spot in my bed
         on my couch, in my car,

    I am sick.

levee

one day I won't feel the need to drink
while you apologize for nothing
we'll rediscover each other
at an all-pronged fork in the road
finally free of this devilish haze

what a cemetery we've conceived

if only we'd stood on two feet
instead of flying nowhere
or lying and submitting

We capitalized on forgetting.

*The beach was a sunny graveyard without him.
The waves would not take her, she understood.
She would have to chart a course.*

*For her new compass, she used a rock from his favorite
seat. A stone she could carry with her always.
Small, but sturdy.*

Something to remind her of their beach...

unnamed lake

That song comes on
somehow I'm singing in a car with friends
driving through the sequoias
planning our future
all smiles and happy tears

such dreams come again

river rock

gaping holes disguised as days mean
I can barely pitch one shade of breath before the next,
hardly lift my legs across my never absent mind

Your name haunts every draping hillside
I can see you, I can hear your voice,
did you ever exist beyond the tinctures of my brain?

I row around the gaping holes,
lest I fall into them headfirst and-
must not fall into them, into you.
must not fall back into you.

I cannot fall back into you.

raindrops

I wish I could shatter
to replace the shards stolen from
your nose
       your fingers
            your toes
all the bits and pieces taken

                how could I?

rusted padlock

I'll still breathe or blink and remember days with you
when I forced myself to think:

                If I drowned in one more drink,
             would it make the winds improve?

I'm trying not to see you
out of the corner of my eye

            hummingbirds fetch sweeter poison
         we feed you snacks to make you smaller

These drugs no longer do the trick

and how thick I must be in the head

to pretend
I'm not grossly underfed

the sick one will sooner be dead.

cinderblock

I've had a second chance or twelve before
their persistent knocking at my door
though I don't leave the light on anymore

they keep on coming back for me
like I'm a frigate
lost at sea

I try to drift
I beg to drown

It's not so easy dragging this one down.

water pipe

I wish the boys had stayed another night

The brute holding my speaker to his big barrel chest
while the bearded Viking snored in the corner
(He has so changed since our last lifetime
even died and reincarnated
somehow maintaining his
exoskeleton like a
recycled solar system)

Strange that the brute held the speaker you got me for
our anniversary
Stoned and finding ways to bridge the gap
I would have let him in my bed

That broad shouldered tattoo proving I lived
before you, his warm skin screaming me in circles,
wet and wandering ever lost and longing for home

I hadn't shaved to my satisfaction or had gotten
too damn drunk and high
Thank God for that or maybe thank nobody
because if I'd sealed the deal
the boys may have stayed another night

lion's bone

You still sweep over my fortress like a
cool, crystallized wildfire
always in unguarded moments,
reaching in,
pulling my heart strings

mood ring

Our last happy night was the opening of Macbeth
you were so proud of me
whistling your standing ovations

you had so much to say
drinking beer and chattering gleefully
in my passenger seat

it reminded me of when we first met

        you flashed your catwalk light at me while they
          rehearsed my lowering string house
           a menace in horn-rimmed glasses

      when we went downtown and that man reached for me and
        you slid your knife to the cuff of your sleeve

      midday in the hotel room we held each other drunkenly
        you wanted to kiss me, but you knew better

your adoration kept me company, so I finally let you in
and for a while we found Neverland,
homemade respite situated safely on the fringe,
but my brainwash kept me chugging kept me smoking
kept me throwing parties for clenched fists
I wanted to keep you, keep your adoration,
keep calling sanctuary, but as these things eroded
into misadventures, you tried the tourniquet
too late to stop the bleeding.

gravel drive

Night succeeds again.

I sit here wondering when you'll come round and
admit you still love me.
I'm beginning to think that you won't
that I'll always be the bad dream
tossing knives and breaking bowls

I hope you find your cabin in the woods.

tonic

I had a dream that they were eating you. I was only a baby and could do nothing about it. I did not remember until midday. I was halfway down to OC. That drive still feels claimed by 21 to 23. If I hadn't made the trip, I might never have recalled the dream. I do not call it a nightmare. I was all dimpled and helpless. Too young to do more than wail and reach out my chubby hands. In the dream I do not call a nightmare, they ate you alive. Gobbled you up like a snack before it dissipated. I did not wake up crying.

holy water

I may not have a mansion waiting
but there still stands
a small house built in your honor

birthstone

I'm sitting in a room with young attractive men,
all talented and intelligent and worthwhile.
I hear them speak of things that ring bells in my ears and
light fires in my eyes. I witness references that stir me
into a familiar, nostalgic hum and rifle through my
tongue twisters to recall a clever tune. I sing it loudly, and am
applauded once again for being quite the good performer.
I work and weave and wind and have mild
revelations by the dozen.

I check my phone and see the date:
Wherever in this wide world you may be without me,
I hope you're having a wonderful birthday, baby.

morning dew

Shot me down like a bird in the sky,
the weapon of choice was the look in your eye.
Each weighed anchor while the other would sleep,
casting all hope down into the deep.
I am lost indeed, as you sail to shore
the North Star won't show her face anymore.
Drifting out further into the night,
abandoning ship as a bird taking flight:
disloyal fiend, I have proven my worth,
and am soon quickly plummeting back down to earth.
Watery grave and familiar sea,
take him safely to land, to sail on without me.

With her head still buried in the sand, Tiger Lily had not really watched Mr. Livingston disappear over the mountain.

The ship had been repaired, her loyal crew stood ready, and the sea was waiting.

The winds were finally in her favor.

HOOK did not know that the crocodile was waiting for him, for we purposely stopped the clock that this knowledge might be spared him: a little mark of respect from us at the end ...

"**Bad form!**" He cried jeeringly, and (with a smile) went content to the crocodile.

-Peter Pan by J.M. Barrie

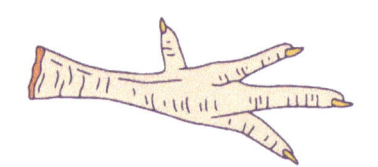

because I'm not as batshit as the broken records told me
I was, or wasn't, or never will be because I'm a proud, decent
person still hoping to
make it out alive.

19

I walked a man
I walked him like a dog
at the end of the road I let him loose
it was not a pleasant conversation.
He shielded
only to yield and be forced to heel like the dog that he is
or the dog that he isn't
or the dog that he never was or never will be, because he's a
proud, decent man and
I'm a batshit broken record.

I talked myself
I talked myself up and down like a fool
at the end of the day I held the phone
It was another one-sided conversation.
I tried
only to rely on the forces of cried,
undried tears that won't
or haven't seemed willing
or haven't felt ready to throw in the towel,
because you can't fix a broken record and
I'm not batshit all on my own.

I found a friend
I found her like a trail
at the end of the line I lost her way
it was an unspoken conversation.
She searched
only to work her way back to learn
how offtrack I had wandered or far down I had fallen
or far forward I'd actually flown on my own,

SPIT SHINE

Maybe if I keep on leaning and spinning and
spilling my coffin onto the lawn
someone somewhere will hear me
coming completely untangled
ditching that handsome last attempt at making it count, or
making a meal unlike well-prepared worm food

making a mark that is less than a burn or a scratch or a
sprinkle of fuming brutality
more than another forgotten encounter
wherein I turn to you dizzy eyed and quite unfamiliar
screaming something or other you didn't see coming

just like the sucker punch still drunk in broad daylight
come on sparkle- that's how you know that I love you.

WOODWARD WAYSAYERS

I'll miss the house on Canyon Creek
it was the last point we still got to be
cousins, and sisters, and friends

before anything else-we were still graces
hopeful and faithful and starved for the fight

suddenly I was the one that might break away sooner, which
is funny now, since
I am mourning an empty house, while it's
them with their children and loved ones and ties

I sit in a tower and talk to the birds
asking if it really was a dream,
                do tell us if you hear something

at some point I could no longer hide
or scurry
or pant
I could only sit
in silence
with the rants reminding me

It comes for me in waves

REDEMPTION

Because at any given time
I still believe these people can be saved, and if that is what
ends up damning me to Hell, well. ..

I suppose I'd get there anyway

CROW'S NEST

There are few worse sounds than pouring
your second to last and hearing the dregs of the bottle
ricochet off of its own insides and yours
makes me want to split my hairs and sell the farm

Helicopters flying so low make the whole building shake
every time it happens, I imagine how it will feel when we
all fall down

Ashes or not there's still gravity, and there will always be
tragedy. Science and what? Circumstances? Humanity?
Plain old rotten, "that's life?"
I feel it in my blind spots. I can see it crush my bones.
an unavoidable impact-hopefully not in the crosswalk,
on my terms and my own information

TURBULENCE

It came for me in waves
like a dungeoned dragon on a swirling, whirling wind
it came for me in waves

LATE BLOOMER

It must be nice to share your scars like party favors
once the bottle spins to me
nobody clears a room like I do

few stay long enough to learn
I'm a good kisser

EFFICIENCY IS KEY

Overnight, I can obliterate a lifetime.

Most of you will think I'm crazy if you don't already.
I have frigidaire moments where the Zhoul mess within
impresses anyone more than it maddens. I cross the border of
chilled conscience and bring aliens back as pets.

It's cute until they tell you they can read grandmother's
prayers and she still catches all those close calls you hoped she
missed because she kicked the bucket.
For a kid with her faith you should know better than that.

When my last evening gown arrives
I'll be too old I'll be too old ...
but old's not dead not door-nailed in
alive means so much more on that drive home than it did
before.

BLAST FROM THE PAST

She told me she hated my hair
I hated her constitution
don't worry

I'll be back before you know it
grabbing bags and taking punches

all the friends I've lost
little anchors at sea

you know who you are
babes and butchers and bad decisions

don't fret

I love the smell of burnt flesh when it deserves it and you
never knew a truer motive than now

I'm sure it's all a thunderstorm
I wish I could take that piece out for everyone's sake
The piece keeping everyone electrified and afraid

for all my lies I've never learned to properly pretend, leave it
onstage, or away from prying fingers pulling triggers

my descent is my legacy
that has always been the problem.

GODMOTHER

I want to tell you who I am
that my insides don't look half as bad
they look worse—
and my heart isn't connected anymore
it's like a voice orbiting me
making false landings
like so many
pretending they'll stay
we have to choose wisely;
speak up without the microphone
a whisper
or a dumbbell
there's no going back.
I hate forgetting what I'd never meant to say
take my guns
leave something that can't hurt the others
if there's anyone left to phase, but
do not feel sorry for yourself
it will make it infinitely harder for
anyone else to feel anything towards you.
Everyone picks sides when someone's life depends on it;
take us as we are now
leave someone better.
Either way, certain bits and pieces reign inevitable
although we try and loop around
this is the circuit
someone has to take the fall, so
why are we still swinging?

                              take the gun. leave the cannoli

LAND HO

I punctured someone's jugular vein in the process
It wasn't my job necessarily, but I remember it felt like a
 good fit at the time
Poison Ivy, or one of the Mermaids?
I could never pick a side

My seafloor awaits me somewhere
maybe the Atlantic with all its bells and whistles
perhaps I was one of Blackbeard's brides?
Or were they mine? Devil or renegade angel?

I lick my chops as the tide rises
I wait to see the sailors on land
kissing sand after months on the water
I wretch and vomit on my sundress
no ships weigh anchor Sunday night

then one day their shipwreck is discovered
with the dutiful captain's
corpse still sitting at his
desk, not expectant and unwilling, and
that night the town sleeps soundly
knowing what they've already known for weeks.

FIGHT FOR WHAT

In some harebrained balderdash memory
I was here before
in the wee hours buying liquor or getting my poor spine
realigned or showing up to the wrong spot...
Buying chewing tobacco for my dugout fiends not yet
eighteen... I've always been important.
People need me for great distances and vital goods
I have great worth when I put my mind to it
When I really put my back into it
when I use elbow grease
that's when you'll notice the difference
that's how my um-star rating goes up
that's how we keep food on the table and our name on the map
If you aren't careful you'll get lost
pretty soon no one's writing you reviews, or
liking your pictures, or
attending your wake

SPIRITUAL INDIGESTION

I lost my head some years ago
my heart soon followed, learning to beat on,
hollowed... and yet, my soul I'd not considered
                a part of me completely splintered.

UNDERTOW

(Often times)
I can hardly keep my head above the water
I try to bob there like an otter
Weighed down from deep below by cinderblocks of long ago,
forged in could have told you so's
and sad old songs nobody knows.

IS THERE A DOCTOR IN THE HOUSE

Oh, the places you'll go
and the people you'll see
all the drinks you will try! (mostly on
me...)

Well, the more that you know
the less you will learn;
more drinks to buy and more bridges to burn.

'N A BOTTLE OF RUM

It's lonely out to sea alone, and hard to sail too,
even with clear skies above & below me ocean blue;
so I must use my siren song to call for worthy crew,
but then my rum-filled pirate's side keelhauls each hitherto.

BATTLESHIP

Oh, sea of mine, oh sea divine:
beloved, I cannot be thine;
I sail, and swim, and sing, and pine,
and on my soul you gladly dine.

It went to all our hearts, I think, to leave them in that wretched state; but we could not risk another mutiny...

-Treasure Island by Robert Louis Stevenson

PIN THE TAIL

If you don't explicitly ask for help
then no one will come back for you
which seems backwards
because you'd think that
someone would realize they were
still carrying your pack down
or even call back up when they find it in their hands
you'd think they might at least take notice once you're
screaming, flailing, falling—
their guilt lives in their relief.

FIRE OR KNIFE

It's not so easy when you're caught
downing the bottle you hit them with
somehow it stays intact through every celebration
you struck clean across their jaws and temples
forgetting
peace and quiet lives at the nape of the neck
cracked skulls lose their sense of humor in the morning
I hoped it was a dream
my knuckles tell me otherwise
broken glass is so appealing in the moonlight,
less so when wedged between fingers and toes
the sun is quite the charmer
if you never stop drinking

I ate them bones and all
now they're stuck between my teeth
somehow the devoured company reminds me of better days
trying to be the class clown
before the jokes landed on me
even when I spit them back out to the crowd
it's like a shameful, daggered boomerang
no one sees but me, and when it
hits me in the head no broken bottle can compare to that
nice slice it keeps taking out while
helping me redecorate my insides

If only I could go back and tell them
never mind I didn't mean it
I could use a good, deep cleaning

I'll take the fire
not the knife

BLACK AND BLUE

Before
back when I was real
the world told me your name
whispered it like a best kept secret
and I ran to tell the others
but
the party had ended
the milk had soured
and no one could be found within a thousand miles.

I came back to carve names in trees
then, decided stone was better
cold and dead
like them

epitaphs were written
I mourned no one and everyone
   your name was there
   and yours
   and yours
some spelled better than others
some happily corrected
others left in place.

I wanted to miss you, but sometimes,
   more than sometimes
I can only miss me
the me before you all came into the picutre and fucked me up

ever the victim
   never the bride.

TRAPEZOID

You'll be happy to hear I do not discriminate
I'll projectile vomit on anything
resin-spat Lamborghini
mom's 89' Taurus
I spew home truths on any dashboard—it's the only place
that keeps me honest

what lucky hunks of metal

OPEN SEASON

He snapped his hungry jaws at me and I'll admit to you, I fled
I'm not used to the attention in this chapter, or this lifetime or
maybe I feel insecure pretending in this outfit

> I DARE YOU
> TO TRY ME
> IN A KNIFE FIGHT

Remembering what it was to feel pretty
either way it won't come easy playing shark bait in the city,
people had better realize

> DROWNING
> ISN'T AN ACT
> ONE TRIES TO REPRISE

I wasn't always afraid though
there were summers when plums and clementines
dictated much more than bruised kunckles
and prosthetic kneecaps

> DID YOU SEE THAT
> OR WAS IT REALLY JUST ME

My roommate's electric eel switched on
and then, swam off and away from its corner
will no one catch it in time?

> MY ROOMMATE DOES NOT HAVE AN EEL
> AND I DO NOT HAVE A ROOMMATE

Syrup sipped through straws at ballerine barbecues
pool parites without any swimming?
Miscommunication can mean an open invitation

> WORDS WERE NEVER OUR FIRST LANGUAGE

PRETEEN GIRLS ARE TERRIFYING
(and we never grow out of it)

It takes a telescope to see my curves
a morphine drip to calm my nerves, but
for a close-up look at open wounds,
you can see my hollows from Saturn's moons.

You can check it out eight days a week.
Nightly showings down at shit-show creek, and
if you'd believe it, it's all for free!
Since all I really want is company...
                    All I really want is company.
                    All I really need is the company.

"If you leave me now you'll rue the day!"
As you've slammed the door, I finally say.
But it's too late now, which is such the theme.
I add, "Well, I'll be fine." Quickly losing steam.

My guardian angel looks on prayerfully:
"Have mercy, my Lord, let the poor girl dream."

BLUE RED VOMIT PARTY

I cut off this and that
they tell me everyone's story like it's my responsibility to
write their shit down

could've been a court reporter
would send flowers to the judge while
taking shots with the jury
throwing daggers of hot love unwanted at that
enigmatic executioner
it's so standard in these trades
as long as you are accurate the people will forigve you-
        THAT IS NOT TRUE

You see the fighting, right? You know.
You served ten thousand suns ago.
You have mutant relatives invested.

break my neck then
you make me wish things onto you that are
already inevitable
your zip-tied revolution of nothing
air-based rights you fringe on freedom
you make me sick
come over and watch the epidemic
you'll sing like a sycophant!
            It's not that hard if you really believe.

WHO THE FUCK IS SIMON, ANYWAY

I saw it coming, Simon.
      Your lessons are something, when you let them sink in.

I listened to your lessons
I spent the whole time thinking,
I told the others not to panic and finish up their drinking.
I told them the important things you said to say, I did:
"Just keep swimming when the tide rises.
Just keep lying when the others start running.
Just keep smiling when the rogue wave hits."

It can be hard to make this lesson stick, and
I do so hope I did.

How did I do, Simon?
Did I give you some respite?
Did I sail through the break?
Did I do just like you said?

Will you help us out aive Simon?

                                             Simon...?

CABIN FEVER

We used a boxcutter that time
it worked just as well, but the
mess we made reminds me still: "you can't open bottled beer
with a screwdriver when the world is upside down!"

It's hard to work my favorite knife with blood in my eyes,
and I'm trying not to laugh, but
you look ridiculous with half your face
hanging to one side
and the other half twisted into that
same wicked grin

You smart ass
don't take my drink
you know I rip the tabs off
yours are the ones turned to the right, or the left—hey!
I'm still choking up tabs from your friendly reminders
I must admit, my gag reflex is a force to be reckoned with

I don't care if your arms were blown to bits by the jukebox
I told you-turn the volume down!
You know that rules are rules, so

        drop down and give me twenty

IT'S 5:00 ALWAYS

I am the girl who walks on walls, demon-eyed
waiting for my next friend to call
(We haven't seen visitors in weeks)
all because I'm losing my touch and can't keep the voices to a
reasonable volume-

-it wasn't all my fault, at least I don't think it was!

it could have been

MASTER CLASS

I like it when you hold me down
it makes me feel the blood in my veins and I know I am alive
it's the only time the look in your eyes still has that icy flame
even now in my imagination
it turns my heart on fire, as the voices
rattle against my skull and tell me:
this memory is all you'll ever have now, kid.

There's nothing left to hold you
no one left to endure
and why should they? Why should you?
But that would be too easy—throwing in the towel.

I wish I could pull the trigger
drag the knife
tighten the cord...
But see that scar keeps me guessing

maybe I am meant for something more than
all this
homegrown deprecation, lightweight perforations

ground me,
don't bury me, baby

2009

Wondering
if that same spot on the sidewalk is there anymore
from the time we both dug concrete holes
that summer it was so hot out the blacktop melted
made it easy to sink right in

better than a mud bath

hot tar knows how to get the dirt out from underneath your
nails
part the hangover from your neatly washed hairs
those smudges of regret really take some doing
and we're a team, you and me
always have been

always will be...

DON'T DRINK THAT

He told me I was the smartest girl he'd ever met.
I told him he was full of shit.
He said: "You're too smart to fall into the usual traps, you
know? You're too good for that."
I took a final drag and replied: "I've been roofied four times."

Then I put it out on the brick wall, blew the smoke up into
the sky, and whispered, "they weren't masterminds."

I spat the rest into his briefcase.

"I'm youth, I'm joy." Peter answered at a venture, "I'm a little bird that has broken out of the egg."

-Peter Pan by J.M. Barrie

The views and opinions expressed in this book are solely those of the author and do not reflect the views or opinions of Gatekeeper Press. Gatekeeper Press is not to be held responsible for and expressly disclaims responsibility for the content herein.

Birdbrain/The Calamitous Chronicle of Mr. Livingston and Tiger Lily

Published by Gatekeeper Press
7853 Gunn Hwy, Suite 209
Tampa, FL 33626
www.GatekeeperPress.com

Copyright © 2023 by Melissa Booey

All rights reserved. Neither this book, nor any parts within it may be sold or reproduced in any form or by any electronic or mechanical means, including information storage and retrieval systems, without permission in writing from the author. The only exception is by a reviewer, who may quote short excerpts in a review.

The cover design, typesetting, and editorial work for this book are entirely the product of the author. Gatekeeper Press did not participate in and is not responsible for any aspect of these elements.

ISBN (paperback): 9781662929458
eISBN: 9781662929465

BIRDBRAIN

poetry by Melissa Booey

Gatekeeper Press

Printed in the USA
CPSIA information can be obtained
at www.ICGtesting.com
LVHW020746051023
760085LV00054B/1119